Illuminations

also by Roger Roloff

***Gathered from the Wild:
Poems of a Wanderer***

The Poetry of Earth

Natural Gifts

Natural Voice
(compact disc)

*For Bryan, also a
lover of the old art —
With warm regards,
Roger
4/11/10*

Illuminations

Roger Roloff

illustrations by Anne S. Ross

The Rhodora Press

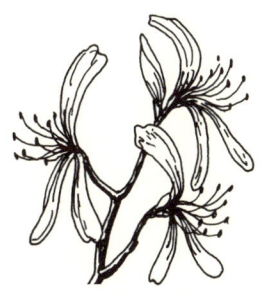

The Rhodora Press
22 Hummel Road
New Paltz, N. Y. 12561

PUBLISHER'S NOTE: This is a work of fiction. Names, characters, places, and incidents are either are the product of the author's imagination or are used fictitiously, and any resemblance to actual persons (living or dead), events, or locales is entirely coincidental.

Text copyright © 2009 by Roger Roloff
All illustrations copyright © 2009 by Anne S. Ross
Back Cover: whorled loosestrife (Lysimachia quadrifolia)

Printed by Maar Printing Service, Poughkeepsie, N. Y., and bound in the United States of America. No part of this book may be reproduced in any form or by any electronic or mechanical means including information storage and retrieval systems without written permission from the publisher. Reviews may quote brief passages, or reproduce illustrations to be printed in a newspaper, magazine, or electronic publication. Otherwise, illustrations may only be reproduced with the permission of the illustrator.

ISBN 978-0-9665367-4-4

*For Wendell Berry, man of reason,
with gratitude and admiration;
and for
the Berry Queen (no blood relation),
for love grown dearer each shared season*

Contents

Foreword ix
Crossing a Covered Bridge 1
Keeping a Sixth Sense 3
Time Travel; or, In a Cold Tub on the Neversink 5
October Light 6
The Blizzard 7
A Song for Songbirds 11
Dreaming Rights 12
One Good Turn Receives Another 14
The Elm-Gatherer 15
January Caprice 17
A Spring Memory 18
A Hardy Orphan 20
A Special Place 21
Love's Labor 29
Homework 30
Indirections; or, Calling on Quaker Ladies 31
Prodigal 34
Out-of-Season Favors 35
Autumn Reckonings 37
Burnout 39
Not Forgotten 44
Outside the Box: a Lone Dissenter 45
Walking into History 47
The Brotherhood 49
The Human Element 50

The Stairway to Heaven 51
October Daybreak 57
Autumn Farewell 58
A Leaf for Hardwoods 59
Clear and Cold 61
In a Black Birch Grove 62
Going for Gaywings 63
Summoning Eliza 66
Mother of All Change 69
The New Age of Dinosaurs 70
Survivors 71
A Tough Old Native 72
The Herb Witch 73
Looking after Wild Wallflowers 76
The Silver Squeak 78
Leaf Dancer 80
By a Frozen Pond 81
A Small White Hope 82
Earth-Centered 83
Stayed by Stars 84
A Flower for All Gardens 85
About the Author and the Illustrator 88

Foreword

In the beginning was the Foreword—or so it always seems. Helpful as this one is intended to be, I will keep it as brief as possible. As readers of *Gathered from the Wild: Poems of a Wanderer*, *The Poetry of Earth*, and *Natural Gifts* know, an important part of my home territory is the Shawangunk mountain range. Though not named in this collection, the Shawangunks provide settings for several poems, among them "October Light," "Dreaming Rights," "In a Black Birch Grove," and "Stayed by Stars." Tangibly and intangibly *Illuminations* owes much to these mountains, inspiring and approachable.

The Catskill Mountains are also near home, thankfully. Certain of their famous trout brooks welcome me every year, not as a fly-fisherman but as a hot and weary blackberry-picker in August or September. The upper reaches of the Rondout Creek and, here in "Time Travel; or, In a Cold Tub on the Neversink," the West Branch of that stream (which rises on Slide Mountain) dependably keep the bath water running between a bracing 55 and 65 degrees Fahrenheit. A dip or longer soak can change a person's outlook on the world, sometimes forever.

The "Catskill shelf" referred to in "Walking into History" must regrettably remain nameless to the reader. As a devoted but I hope discreet forager, I have to protect sources—human and vegetable—requiring anonymity. (For more on the forager's art, which has much in common with the poet's, see "Indirections; or, Calling on Quaker Ladies.") "Going for Gaywings" takes place by a trout brook which, however, can be named. It is the Vernooy Kill, a Catskill tributary locally prized if less widely known. Upstream its cold, clear water flows by the site of Potterville, also mentioned in the poem and now only a ghost on older maps.

I have called this book *Illuminations* because the poems were inspired by natural light in some of the countless ways it appears; by moments of clarification, recognition, understanding, or insight in people close to Nature; or by a combination of these literal and figurative lights. I haven't aimed to depict what might be termed traditional religious illumination, although the book necessarily places high value on enlightenment through Nature. This begins with "Crossing a Covered Bridge," which metaphorically elaborates poetic vision shaped by traditional form and changing yet ever-renewed Earthly scenes.

Thereafter individual poems occur in seasonal order: thus the glow of "October Light" precedes "The Blizzard," which yields to spring music in "A Song for Songbirds," summer's "Dreaming Rights," and so on. Occasionally two or three juxtaposed poems deal—not always strictly by the calendar—with aspects of the same season: examples here are "The Herb Witch," "Looking after Wild Wallflowers," and "The Silver Squeak." In contrast, some poems—"Earth-Centered" and "Outside the Box: a Lone Dissenter"—are not bound to a particular season, appearing like uncharted comets or asteroids. There are, moreover, poems which mark seasons gone awry, with larger implications: "Mother of All Change" and "The New Age of Dinosaurs." In short, the succession of poems, though seasonal, shows the considerable variety found in rings of an old oak: also a natural measure of light.

Finally—and lest anyone suppose that reading *Illuminations* precludes cracking a smile or laughing out loud—let's not forget that light can and does break through darkest thoughts and graveyard scenes. Those cases may be more memorable for such moments, in fact. To pretend otherwise falsifies the richness and complexity of life. Or, to illustrate the point in rhyme:

> In making sense of life on Mother Earth,
> I use in part the ways of song and mirth.

Illuminations

Crossing a Covered Bridge

A different world waits on the other side;
the dirt road from the highway told me that.
I paused before the span few travelers tried
and sensed what they perhaps had marveled at:
an aura, built to last with old hand tools,
expressing transport through the country air
now lost to all but maverick trade schools.
Unpainted walls bore witness to the wear
of storms and sun-bleach, and could not quite hide
(some boards were missing) hemlock lattice-work
that kept unbowed the bridge's native pride.
Inside were carved—call it a builder's quirk—
a name and date as on a master's art
so formed to carry on its maker's time
yet show how well he saw the open part
which frames a landscape always in its prime.
Each measured footstep toward this living scene
revealed—enlarged—much more that drew me on:
clouds lifted to unveil the jutting green
of mountains as a thrush sang, then was gone.
Cornfields and new-mown hay filled bottomland
that grew and stretched to meet the river's edge,
while quickened paces brought me near its sand
and bankside perfume from a wild rose hedge.
By then I'd reached and hurried through the frame
into the picture—as an eager lover
is moved by sudden passion he can't tame
except by finding all he can discover.
Oh, that was many well-spent Junes ago,
and still I'm pulled back in the best and worst
of seasons, seeking ever more to know

and learn from—still a lover, as at first.
The covered bridge stands ready now to train
five senses with its clear and steady focus
on a great blue heron fishing in fall rain,
or sun-teased petals of a purple crocus.
These days I cross as slowly as I can.
The bridge and old road (innocent of gravel)
have taught me to. And I've no better plan
than cultivating wisdom by foot travel.

Keeping a Sixth Sense

Urged on by light-green blossoms of spicebush,
my love and I walk to a flower show
our old friend April holds each year to push
out winter's drabness for the purple glow
hepaticas display, spring beauties' veins
of pink, trout lilies' yellow flashing bright.
For these we look beyond our aches and pains
to feel with all wild lives the season's might
grip us: an inborn sense of primal wonder
true Earthly children never can outgrow,
that no machines or picture-screens can plunder.
And though we know our ramble may not slow
the rush with which man's war on Earth is waged,
we're grateful to be otherwise engaged.

Time Travel; or, In a Cold Tub on the Neversink

When summer days grow hot and hotter
deep memories of mountain water
propel me upstream to a pool
that always keeps an ancient cool.
It's no primordial urge to spawn
which grips my thoughts and drives me on,
just inner need, less old but true,
to feel full-length that world anew
which modern ways cannot improve.
The brook's no artificial groove,
but frees my form in its own, clear,
and makes the very atmosphere
original as streambed rocks,
slow-chiseled from great bluestone blocks.
A traveler in its current time
need only float or drift to prime
the mind to touch eternity,
where past and future streams agree
in one uninterrupted flow.
I'll save that present here to know,
when life piles burdens I must shed
downstream to lift my heart and head.

October Light

Illumination of deep maple woods
that blinding beams of mid-July can't give,
that stirs us with fall's old imperative
to wander in rich-colored solitudes,
grant us—before wild winds begin the noise
of tumbling, swirling leaves and end the glow
of harvest time—one slow, blest day to know
this ripened beauty's momentary poise;

so that when winter's cold hands, swift by dark,
strip all the glorious raiment overhead
and strew it on bleak landscape left for dead,
they cannot kill what memory will spark,
yes! even on December's longest night:
the mind's eye in a forest filled with light.

The Blizzard

I smelled the snowstorm coming.
Cold dampness filled a sky
turned milky gray and numbing
to any passerby.
The sawbuck I worked at
stood foot-deep in piled white
already, though spring sat
a week away in spite
or jest on calendars.
Sighing, I knew each stack
of logs would wear new furs
before I could get back.
As dusk's low rays were cast,
into this dreary scene
a pair of wrens flew fast
and landed, caught between
two seasons and two days—
it mattered little where
they came from, heaven's strays.
And then they plied the air
with singing, sweet and strong
enough indoors for me
to hear each varied song.
Meanwhile but quietly
first flakes began to fall.

Night hid the singers and
their dwindling notes, grown small
and smaller as the land
itself was muffled by
a cloak of frozen wool
which smothered every cry.

Yet when the sky is full
to bursting, winds that died
an hour ago may rise,
reborn, and swell white tide—
mounting to terrorize
the countryside by force
which made old pine boughs moan
and crack without remorse.
All night my home was blown
into another world,
a high sea by its sound,
whose huge waves surged and swirled
as terra firma drowned.

I could not say dawn broke
but rather struggled higher,
like scattered, distant smoke
above a doubtful fire.
The blizzard's constant drone
was not all that I *heard*,
however; welcome tone
came from a wily bird
that found the kitchen vent
for shelter in a wall
where wasps once came and went,
nesting from May till fall.
His shy spouse answered, trilling
more softly in wren-speech—
which coaxed a new song, filling
space out of snow's wild reach.
So back and forth they chanted
until he, noticing
a lull the wind had granted,

flew off to eat or bring
small morsels, snatched from suet
I'd hung, to feed the mate
that did not fly out to it,
but seemed content to wait.
Or forced—I wondered then—
as snowbound afternoon
grew gray, and just the wren
that varied his bright tune
dared to take wing. Replies,
trilled softer still, were weak
as last daylight which tries
to find a cloud-capped peak.
I felt a chilly doubt
myself, as scant light faded
and high drifts ranged about,
that I'd get out unaided.

Again night's curtain fell,
and in redoubled rage
the storm howled on to tell
me of the new Ice Age
plastering windowpanes
and sealing every door.
Yet next day lusty strains
of birdsong rang once more;
both wrens snatched suet bites
out of the blizzard's teeth.
Meantime I cleared white heights
my bowed roof groaned beneath,
and shoveled on till, growling,
my stomach called for lunch.
Gone was the tempest's howling,

I realized, as the crunch
of packed snow underfoot
resounded; and mere flakes
were all the sky's output
could add to my backaches.
So furious was my labor
that, as the storm went slack,
I'd missed the wind's sharp saber
dropping behind my back!
Relieved, I ate and napped.

Yet one scene in my dream
chilled me on waking: trapped
by winter's icy gleam,
a pair of wrens fought still
against a swift, cold fate.
I watched and listened till
the spent day lay in state,
then through the frigid night
thought of those birds—a clever,
bare ounce of feathered might—
and of our joint endeavor
to see spring in at last.
I'd hear their tunes whenever,
I hoped. So winter passed.

But not its power to sever,
as lost song-times amassed
days stretching into never.

A Song for Songbirds

Who dares to oversleep at spring's green height?
Many a shade tree's crown of new leaves trembles
as breeding music's heavenly host assembles
and wild-tuned choirs enchant dark Earth to light.

Their ancient love songs tell the season's speed
and reach, and celebrate a world grown fecund
beyond what humankind has known or reckoned
of art's old power for order born of need.

Yes, songbirds' lives are short and hard, the norm
forced by a wilderness of narrow choices.
And yet the miracle of this singing swarm
that's spanned eons but even now rejoices
is built on strong and varied solo voices:
still striving, thriving, staying true to form.

Dreaming Rights

The patch is berry heaven this July.
I've never seen it bluer, or so black
where night-dark huckleberries sweetly vie
for more room in my mouth or bulging pack.
There's too much for one man to taste and savor!
Each handful proves this harvest is unique,
and bushes—picked and unpicked—start to waver
and dance in a dazzling vision. I grow weak,
at length retreating to the rustling shade
five oaks have spread, and sit to breathe new scent
sweetfern and milkweed blossoms jointly made.
The only other sound is birdsong lent
by towhees, prairie warblers, yellowthroats:
my old companions in high summer's labor.
Though resting, I am keen on making notes
myself which all the years as their good neighbor
bring surely like ripe, clustered fruit to mind.
But now this priceless bounty's grown so great
my eyes glaze quickly as I contemplate
wild crops gathered, stored, endlessly combined.
So many buckets filled to overflowing—
and yet most of these berries hang till dried
by August's oven, and may cling when blowing
snowstorms have blown me to a warm fireside....
Past heavy eyelids I still spy blue fingers
and shirt-stains where spilled juice like dark ink lingers.
And while my back and neck and knee-joints ache
and rising dampness turns the late-day sun
bloody-hot, those aren't reasons to forsake
well-chosen work before it is half-done.
I often wonder if the job chose me,
in fact, this happy blend of toil and fun.

I couldn't wish for better either way
in this world or another, if I'm free
to seize the dream that lets a worker play.
The mountain's towhees must have dreamt it, too;
they've earned the ancient privilege, I'd say,
long homing here to make that dream come true.
Enrapt or dozing off, I hear their song,
in accents pealing from the heart's deep core,
proclaiming with resolve grown no less strong
that freedom and free voice worth fighting for.

One Good Turn Receives Another

My footsteps brought me from fall's russet wood
to pavement winding up a round hilltop,
treed sparely for the headstone neighborhood.
The long, wide view invited me to stop
for lunch. Yet soon lined stubble in the valley
marked shadows sliding nearer, and I watched
a slanting shower fill the river's alley.
Cold rain it was; but then the storm hopscotched,
and shafts of light dried me and old lined stones.
My back to one, I ate atop the place
where some farsighted member of my race
slept soundly. And to thank his thoughtful bones—
as rain veered back to be that day's play-master—
I left them sunshine in a long-rayed aster.

The Elm-Gatherer

A kind of undertaker I know saves
his winter days to gather long, gray bones
of standing, barkless elms you often see
on roadsides—tall and gaunt in rigor mortis—
until the rot of ages brings them down.
Not that he waits so long, but goes to work
with crosscut saws once lengthwise splits have creased
those rangy skeletons which loiter not
near human heads but with bystanding crowns,
survivors waiting open-armed for spring.
He doesn't want the trees that birds made homes in,
nor does he bother with old, punky trunks
whose soggy wood held rain (now ice) too well
for any flame to start a useful fire.
And sometimes while he carves up carcasses
of windfalls he recalls tired reasons not
to waste his strength on elms, he told me once:
"Won't split, smoke more than burn, *will* rot and fast.
All true," he said, deadpan, "and all false too:
you must know when to cut and how to store them.
A newly sawn green elm cannot be split
with ease by hand or even by machines;
crossed grain is at the slaughtered heart of it
and won't release its stubborn grip for years—
maybe not till a fungus wins it first.
Far better that it drop its peeling skin
and stand naked in natural death for sun
and wind and rain to add their seasoning
until deep cracks have lined the graying corpse.
Then tough grain's lost its grasp and shows where wedges
or blades from mauls and axes can break through.

But stacks of elm bones will not keep outdoors
and need dry shelter only woodsheds give—
not crammed piles smothered under clammy tarps.
For even soaked limbs you'd swear couldn't burn
might yet if given months and room to dry:
you can't reduce elm to a formula.
The whole job's not a business but an art
for educated guessers not afraid
to laugh loudly and long if they guess wrong."
He laughed himself at that—this lone, free man
who with sharp hand tools patiently transformed
troves others scorned—and left me with a song:

"When elm logs struck together ring
like bowling pins' bright, high-pitched ping,
then watch the fire these sticks will build
for lambent blue which seems distilled
from memories of summer flowers
the tree stood by all blooming hours—
as if somehow heartwood intuits
and burns to show a patch of bluets
or pure drifts of forget-me-nots
that plant a heaven in wet woodlots.
This cool light is the deeper reason
to seek and find what in death's season
still keeps a vision here, sublime
in bloom, as blue flames shimmer and climb."

January Caprice

Caught by white fury's sudden scare,
I hurried through the blinding squall
which worried cracks in a woodshed's wall.
The eaves I reached with snow-capped hair.

Cold heaven's surprise gave fresh meaning
to winter's hidden bag of tricks
and to my dwindling store of sticks,
once rafter-tall, now slumped and leaning.

Yet minutes after snow began
the quiet tempest turned and ran,
leaving behind what sunshine flooded:
a land in ermine, diamond-studded—
and a well-worn stovepipe I still knew
by its ragged, trailing scarf of blue.

A Spring Memory

Gold blazing in blue East,
our rising star reclaimed
land winter only leased
and had for too long tamed.
Packed snow and icy teeth
above a growing brook
soon lost their solid look
and swelled the flood beneath.
Swamp maples in fresh mud
stretched long arms heavenward,
showing each fat red bud
to any early bird.
The air was not the same:
though perfumed with wood smoke
it echoed with the croak
of peepers' song by name.
Sapsuckers' rat-tat-tat
tattooed a tree nearby,
but suddenly the cry
a hawk screamed silenced that.
The brief chill died, and spring
resumed its merry pace
as a mockingbird filled space
with a medley on the wing.
I gladly gathered all
these signs of life I'd missed,
and others, too, since fall
had whittled down the list;
and though the yearly war
that spring could not help winning
seemed well past its beginning,
fierce battles lay in store.

Yet none of those that morning
roused me from winter sleep;
it was the sun's fair warning
of a vow it meant to keep
then, March the twenty-second,
which thrilled me to the core
with a world that shone and beckoned
me barefoot out the door.

A Hardy Orphan
—*for B. A. P.*—

There is a flower I watch for every summer,
an orphan in a garden I call mine
and yet no random wildling or newcomer
but planted so the old bed has some spine.

Who left the flower behind I never knew,
though I can sense a certain well-bred taste
surviving in the hybrid salmon hue
on stems that climb for cuttings to my waist.

Not just for subtle scent this flower grows
do I dote on it, but because—in spite
of browsing deer and roots last winter froze
or buds which rabbits find a rare delight
or all its years may otherwise impose—
it has prevailed and is a lovely rose.

A Special Place

"Maureen, let's buy that little farm up north."

"Which one?"

         "You know—twelve acres on the lake.
The house our neighbor Jack fixed up and wants
to sell because—"

         "Oh yes, he lost his wife."

"And 'golden' years—barely eight months, before…
Well, anyhow, he's ready now to sell—
he told me yesterday—and privately
to folks he knew would take good care of it.
I'm certain he's not out to get top dollar."

"No, no, he wouldn't be—poor lonely man.
He charged too little when we stayed a week
back in the spring of—was it 'ninety-two?"

"Or 'ninety-three."

         "And found the painted trilliums."

"And lady's-slippers."

         "And swarms of black flies.
But even so it was a splendid time.
Remember, Phil, loons calling through the sunset?"

"And after."

         "Well, it was remote."

"Still is,
Jack says, though he's had power for six years.
That surely must have cost our thrifty friend;
no neighbors for a country mile, I bet."

"Except wild ones the state park sends his way.
We know about coons crisscrossing the roof
and black bears rummaging through garbage cans.
No stopping their loud midnight parties, right?"

"Unless a rifle dropped some revelers.
I'd rather keep meat scraps not in our compost
but frozen where they won't rot, and each month
donate them to the town dump's safe deposit."

"Very funny."

                "You know we do it now
and it works well. Our eighty-seven acres
are bounded everywhere by settlements,
so wildlife looks on our land as its own.
I'm not complaining, mind you. Grouse and turkeys
in woods—as well as fox and deer and rabbits—
hayfields with meadowlarks and bobolinks,
grain crops and pastures with their sparrow nests:
all these are bonuses, don't you agree?"

"Well, yes—"

                "So living up north wouldn't change
much but our acreage. It might be time,
I think, to sell the livestock or cut back
to chickens, two milk cows, a few meat hogs.

My head and yours can't get much grayer."

                                                "But
we're not decrepit by a long shot, as you
should know—up early hunting deer and turkeys,
up late coon-hunting. Geezers don't do that.
Besides, I thought you liked to plow with horses.
What's really on your mind, Phil?"

                                      "Mainly people—
too many of them, too many telling me
how I should live. Last week I overheard
the usual potshots at 'those smelly farms'—
as if manure's *unnatural*. Imagine
that squeaky-clean crowd living by a feedlot!
I'm tired of yahoos' looking down on me,
that's what. Don't they know where their food comes from?
And there's the tax increase shot from the hip
while government pays small farmers lip service.
Why deal with that the rest of my born days?
Then Jack came by for coffee, making sure
I was the first to hear about his plan
and, well, a golden opportunity,
it seems, that might not come our way again.
Yes…so I slept on this, dreaming all night
of that special place we could make our own.
I'd hunt and fish, you'd finally have time
for flower-gardening, we'd grow the crops
we needed to get by and nothing extra.
No meddling townies poaching on our lives!
Just woods and lakes and peaks forever wild.
Maureen, I think we owe it to ourselves."

"It's tempting, I admit it's mighty tempting.
But what makes it so special? Tell me that.
No people, or not many? Views unspoiled
by dirty hands of commerce? Our four hands
are soiled from good old trade we learned from Nature.
Remember last fall's third-grade visitors?
They didn't want to leave, and begged their teacher
to bring them back in spring; and when they came,
that bug-eyed towhead—I'm thinking Dave's his name—"

"Oh yes, the one who helped me fertilize."

"—piped up and said, 'You make the dead earth live.'"

"Spoken like a born poet."

                "Or a preacher.
The longer I considered, it's hard not
to be the slightest bit religious, Phil,
about the work we do. We test topsoil
for minerals and pH and so forth
but can't explain how deeply it's alive.
It's Nature's secret. We can play along,
or not, yet either way we know it's true
and, yes, miraculous."

                "Amen to that."

"And let's not be so modest to forget
thirty-six years we've spent building our soil.
This place was full of weeds when we got here.
We've made it prosper, but it took hard work
and needs our loving care to stay that way.

It's special for the simple reason we
have thrived by trusting Nature's ways and rhythms.
Take us away from this long partnership
and we will suffer just as much as topsoil.
With all due sympathy to Jack, I can't
live out the dream he lost up north and lose
the dream we've planted ourselves in so well.
I know we need wild lands to let *minds* roam,
if nothing else, but more and more we need
good earth that's *better* for our living there.
My sermon's done."

"Not wasted on deaf ears.
Mine are still ringing in this hard front pew."

"Scoot over, rascal. Is the coffee ready?"

"Almost. Care for some service berry pie?"

"You baked it?"

"Who else? See the lattice-top?"

"My dear, someday you'll make a fine housewife."

"Watch out for my bruised ego; it's still smarting
from your fine speech."

"Touché. You gave up fast."

"How can a farmer argue with his sunlight?
It's true to life and undeniable."

"What does that make you?"

                      "Moonlight, I expect.
Seductive, maybe; charming in its way,
but just a pale reflection of full truth."

"And nothing you'd grow crops with…Wait a minute!
We're getting sidetracked. Why'd you bake the pie?
Come on, confess."

                      "A special treat, I guess."

"You guess? I think I get the picture now.
You hoped I'd want to nest in north woods, too,
were counting on it. Isn't that the truth?"

"I honestly don't know. I do know this:
never to take your yea or nay for granted.
So, undecided as I was, I showed
Jack's offer in the best light that I could;
and if it stood up to your light of day,
well, then, I'd be content. But either way
I wanted you to have the final word."

"I don't know what to say…Thank you, for starters.
But why'd you talk as if you had no doubts?"

"I thought *you* might. What better way to flush
them out—you understand? You spoke your mind."

"And heart."

"I need them both. And anyway,
how can the moon make do without the sun?"

"You're switching metaphors."

"Not much. Besides,
I wasn't sold on everything I dreamed.
The thought of starting from scratch at my age,
and watching this farm cease to be a farm—
it all got painfuller the more I pondered.
We'll keep on doing our level best right here
and try to smile past folks who have no clue
to the real value of land they think they own."

"But don't leave out young Dave."

"I won't, I can't.
Young bucks need years to win their land and herd.
Some never do. We'll have to hope he does."

"Aren't you the poet today? Now, while we're waiting,
could you please pass the coffee and the cream?"

"Of course. As soon as we fully enjoy
the newest heavenly phenomenon:
a solar eclipse—by tickling, then by kissing."

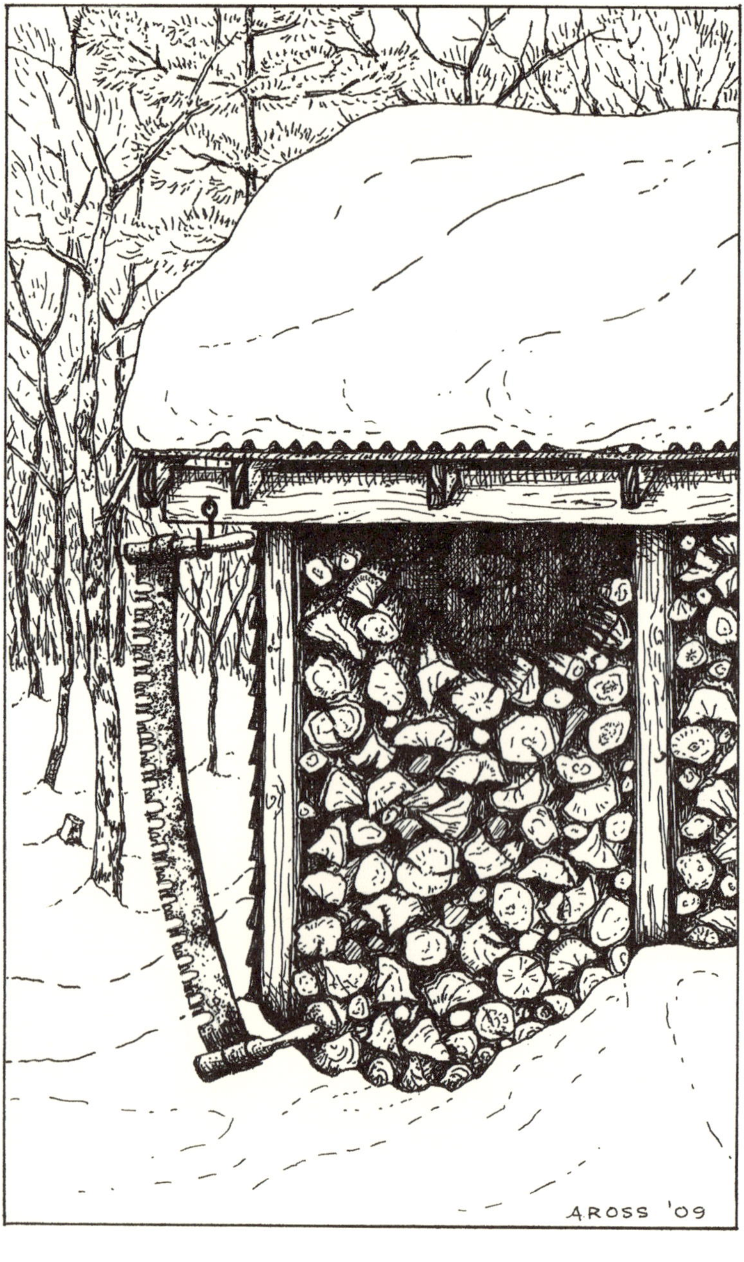
A.ROSS '09

Love's Labor

Our long two-person crosscut saw's at rest.
For one more time it's helped us stay abreast
of winter and most of the year ahead.
And though billows of white surround the shed,
snow-floods don't keep us from woodpiles inside,
whose warmth outlasts cold waves of wintertide.
How many hours we pulled that five-foot blade
and heard the smooth and rhythmic notes it played
upon rough trunks of ash and elm and oak!
We know our work will all go up in smoke,
but that has not stopped us from loving it.
The season only is itself when lit
by fires we and old sawteeth build together
to live in harmony with wintry weather.

Homework

My human neighbors, gone elsewhere for work,
have left me with a clearing April day.
I tend the woodstove, watch the coffee perk.
The not-quite-fix-it shop across the way
is silent, so instead of engines' roar
a phoebe sings, and then a fine song sparrow.
Though barefoot I'm drawn out the southward door
to feel spring's muse work best upon my marrow.

Earth's home-grown business progresses well,
snowdrops and crocuses have stood to tell.
Spring peepers pipe, "Oui! oui!" as small bees arc
toward my plum tree: too soon for blooms' white spell,
but not for me, still, leaning on its bark,
to be here in this season and to mark.

Indirections; or,
Calling on Quaker Ladies
(A Family Portrait, Drawn circa 1954)

Suppose you see a forager stroll past,
one summer day. You wouldn't ask flat out
where he is bound and what he's looking for.
He's not about to broadcast his trade secrets.
Most likely you would get a guarded smile,
perhaps a thoughtful glance away and onward,
and presently sly but good-natured blarney:
"Oh, I'm just visiting some Quaker ladies."
And chances are if he let you come with him,
he'd wink at hundreds as you passed them by.
Yet if you followed him from farther off
and watched him stop, intently looking right
or left, you still might not find really why.
Eventually you'd lose him or give up.
It's always like that with the best of them.
I well remember my old uncle Rourke,
who taught me all I know about the art,
and some tricks I've forgotten down the years.
We'd wander out, each with a paper bag:
his for fresh herbs and greens and mine for mushrooms.
As we wove in and out of woods, it seemed
he stopped by chance to stare hard at the ground,
his big nose pointing like an Irish setter's.
And moments later came his eager question,
"Now, which bag shall we add to, Russell-boy?"
I'd hesitate until he gave a clue,
sometimes, and oftener than not guess wrong.
I'd hear a chuckle or a burst of laughter
escape like unexpected crowing then,
but didn't take offense since he confessed

how much he'd learned by trial and error, too.
And there'd be times (surprise!) we'd use both bags.
Once when I zeroed in on big morels,
he nodded, smiling, as his walking stick
touched chickweed and pale violets by them.
I never got the feeling, though, that he
knew any more than I did what we'd find.
He simply read the landscape like a book
he loved returning to once more with pleasure.
He'd quote from books, too, when it served his purpose:
to feel at home in Nature's wild cropland
"so that the taste of mustard greens takes in
as well the creaking oak, the flicker's cry,
the brook that bathes marsh marigolds nearby."
He last said that, oh, thirty years ago
at least, but how it brings back his warm voice!
They both have stuck with me, I'm pleased to say.
And his main point stays true: wild learning's open
to all; it's our great Earthly heritage.
Some have an inborn knack, like Uncle Rourke,
who cracked that code his whole life for sheer joy.
"This outdoor school beats any other kind—
right, Russ?" he asked, and we would laugh together.
Not that he *ever* let on it was easy,
just that tuition for each course was free.
You learned by finding the answers yourself—
and nobody should hope to get them all
(how stale our dreams and this old world would grow).
He'd only hint about cute Lily Day,
who kept a summer place along his road,
or mention Cress and Columbine's rock-climbing.
That was his way of having fun with facts.
It played with you and life and gave him space—
his own apart, communing cheerfully

with what most people these days overlook.
I think of him just so: not really gone
but gladly joined to Earth forevermore—
and flirting with those pretty Quaker ladies.

Prodigal

Back from an all-night binge on wine-dark seas,
a foggy star, hung over and slow-rising,
revives in fits, matched by a fitful breeze,
and near noon tries some serious botanizing.

In one square mile his beams feed old palm trees
and heather heights, make fuchsia hedges sprout
all year, find orchid nooks which only bees
and he will ever know or care about.

Soon he slips off behind the scenes, inciting
low, muscled clouds to let loose their dark brawn.
He'll send a rainbow for effect as fighting
winds down, then hide himself—sly leprechaun—
once more in faery mists made by the ton
to show (who doubts it?) he's Ireland's true sun.

Out-of-Season Favors

I don't know who might be more daft,
my neighbor, new and city-bred,
or I who simply should have laughed
when he took it into his head—
despite a hundred two degrees
in shade—to cut down four dead trees.

He thought he'd done me one large favor,
I gathered by his tone and smile;
I should have been not nice but braver
and told him it would be a while—
December's sun is much less hot—
before his elms reached my woodlot.

He feared the bark-poor, tall quartet
would likely hit his house broadside.
But that sat north, and who would bet
dead trees arched toward the sun collide
by falling back, away from it?
This strained good sense—more than a bit.

Still, he was right about the wood:
bone-dry, a prize for sharp-eyed poachers
in any season—understood.
I didn't like to let encroachers
make off with one full, uncut cord,
and so to claim the warm reward

resigned myself to pails of sweat
I knew would be the heat wave's price,
hard labor I'd not soon forget.
Yet overnight the weather's vise
somehow got loose—no answered prayer
of mine, but autumn in the air

surprising me just in the nick
of time with two cool days, a fact
I nonetheless called heaven's trick:
to blow in what this summer lacked—
not dog days, ragweed, goldenrod,
but a sly and welcome act of God.

Autumn Reckonings

It's getting hard to find a less-traveled lane.
I thought I had—one mid-fall day, mid-week—
as our great ball of fire began to wane.
Woods glowing red and yellow could but speak
in dry tones hoarsely by the unmapped road,
which seemed deserted, and to me alone
complained that they'd lost half their summer load.
I sympathized in silence—as I'm prone
to do—then farther on saw shiny sticks
below a small black box: a sight too odd,
in truth, to be ascribed to Nature's tricks.
Five paces more made plain a tall tripod
and camera and soon the man they served,
who nearly backed into the gear and me,
so hard he stared upslope where treetops curved
to meet a crest amid their rocky sea.
"Must be the peak," he blurted—this by way
of saying hello, I guessed, and watched him stare.
Smiling, I ventured that the summit lay
northward and gestured cautiously up there.
"No, no," he countered, "it's the leaves, you see.
They're at their best." Nodding as in assent,
I asked, winking, "But would the trees agree?
They might be grieving for the green they've spent."
He mimed a mirthless laugh, then turned to face
the toy without which he would have no trade,
no picture retailing this wilder place.
And this at last would hang retouched, remade
to tame rough parts (for I recalled his craft)
to smooth perfection, though a trifle bland—
as if poor, homely hardwoods, understaffed,
beg make-up's bourgeoisie to lend a hand.

They say a picture's worth a thousand words,
but all I've heard his earn are "ah" and "oo."
You'd get more sense from love-sick mockingbirds.
Perhaps such praise is really made up, too,
responding to an old and common need
to put great Nature safely on display:
soft autumn ripeness staying its dire deed
of murder in cold blood to serve decay.
Not that the seller of half-truth would change
his trick photography to something better.
Fall past the peak is not for him—too strange
to dwell on death, in spirit or in letter.
And yet he's seen it coming, or what *are*
leaves losing hold, and those that did, about?
To help their quickly passing beauty bar
dark thoughts is all his art can be, no doubt:
he knows his buyers' taste. How much fear hides
behind his small supply, their large demand!
I turned back to the old dirt lane that guides
my footsteps well yet lacks a name or brand.
The dying year in untold griefs and glories
still beckoned, not perfection's monolith;
I wandered on to learn and feel those stories
and find true, singing lines to tell them with.
I'd like to think the universe is whole
but never hope to know it without flaws:
only to reconcile my reasoning soul
to power beyond my grasp that made its laws.

Burnout

Two hours gone since he cursed and slammed the door.
No reasoning when his words are lightning bolts
thrown wildly at our life in general.
They won't electrocute those foxes, though,
or jolt Rhode Island Reds to life again.
He surely must have fixed the fence by now.
I'm sorry, Alice; it's no way to treat
the aunt we haven't seen since we got hitched:
you're unexpected sunshine in December.
Don't mind my chatter. I'll dust while you're knitting.
I'd like to blame Paul more—but then I'm caught,
remembering how sixteen years up here
have made his moods as changeable as skies
that promise full sun but deliver hailstorms.
We knew the risks we'd face from the beginning
but hadn't guessed how they might wear us down.
I only saw a half-cleared mountain knob
that seemed to say, "Here you can be yourselves."
Paul must have heard those dream-words just as clearly
and whispered, "Evelyn, this looks like home,"
then lifted me so gently for a kiss.
We walked the bounds like children in a trance,
taking in this new world from every angle
and some outside stone walls and corner stakes:
a spring still higher up, a rocky ledge
off west, and—worth the long, steep hike next day—
a lake stretched out five hundred feet below
we called our fish-shaped fjord, blue as Paul's eyes.

We cut the knob's white pines to fix the house
and barn, then fenced them with red cedar, dead
for years and lying in the sugar bush.

We needed help to get the windmill up
but not much since, and neither has the wind,
raking our leaves each fall into the bargain.
Those words, you say, drew pictures on my postcard?
With power and water to spare, we had it made—
or so we liked to think, with fingers crossed.
Trouble came soon after, killing one dream.
Parasites loved sheep, penned or grazing freely
in big high pastures where some wandered off,
found oftener by coyotes than our collie.
Paul bottle-fed more than his share of newborns
when ewes kept butting weaker lambs away,
and still they died: expensive fertilizer.
Five years we tended the sick, shrinking flock,
then sent survivors to the slaughterhouse.
You don't remember this? I thought I'd written....
That left the chickens, half a dozen pigs,
and two milk cows to keep us company,
but mainly garden chores have ruled our lives.
We never guessed three fallow, sloping acres
for produce and some flowers would make us servants.
I'm not complaining, since the plants grew well
and both plots look out on the lake's long gorge,
a cool place to rest your eyes on dog days.
Paul teases me sometimes when I stare off:
"Now, Evvie, you can't eat the view, you know."
I laugh along with him, but more and more
I wonder if that's what we've gone and done.
Nobody can resist this eagle's view
of Earth or soon forget it, Paul included.
(Men are the biggest dreamers, I have learned.)
He built a bench so we could bask in flames
of dawn or dusk and watch night wheel its lights.
Our home here is the height of our adventure

and feeds us, body and soul, year in, year out.
Tell me, who'd farm this hill for crops alone?
One village market day that simple fact
hit me between the eyes when folks passed up
our lettuce for the picture-perfect kind,
developed with chemicals we don't use.
Or cabbage-worms showed up on cauliflower,
so Paul took nervous customers aside
and faced down tough skeptics by joking, partly:
"Eat the worms—better for you than bug sprays!"
We might lose buyers, but not our sense of humor.
Well, market days *are* trying, usually:
first picking everything a day ahead,
then trucking it eight miles before the crack
of dawn, no matter what tricks weather plays.
Ten hours running we cope with restless crowds,
eyes beaming one thought only: more for less.
By twilight we tote up cash with tired hands—
at last not overworked. The day-old produce,
wilted like us, we lug back to the truck.
Sometimes the extra hands that we had longed for—
those tiny, stillborn dreams—flash through my mind,
and I'm relieved they missed this drudgery.
(Forgive me, I'll be all right in a moment.)
Oh! Alice, *this* is how we've limped along:
the truth that lurks between the lines I dropped you.

You never had our native chestnut trees
in Calgary, right? Yes, we have a few....
Once I was walking off a gloomy mood
in our high woods and found a chestnut stub,
roots sprouting suckers by the rotten trunk,
long dead from blight the new growth gets in time.
These roots, I swore, were wrapped around our future:
they can't make healthy trees but won't quite die.

I thought of them last June when, suddenly,
as if a spell hung *catkins* on those suckers,
my flowers sold out on every market day,
or nearly did, and kept on through October.
The city people couldn't get enough,
in pots or fresh-cut, some in fancy vases.
Cars even climbed our steep, old gravel road
and took home loads of dust along with dahlias.
The flowers had saved us and the farm—and yet
no matter how Paul's words chimed with my joy,
his eyes looked less triumphant than resigned,
as though somehow another dream had faded.
He wouldn't dare admit it, but he's jealous.
Damn human pride! the blight that never leaves.
If only he'd realize how much I love
him *and* the farm in spite of all the grief.
And now—now I'm afraid he loves me less.
We can't quit when our hard work's paying off!
I won't be owned by monstrous new machines
that grind profits from human hearts and minds!
The living we have grown is our true life
on this old earth that makes us sweat to earn it.

It's winter—no season to throw out seeds
or dig up bulbs waiting for blossom-time.
Our blooming's not done either, I'm convinced.
We're planted here as deeply as the dream
that caught us off guard, flowering late but well.
By rights I should be laughing at this joke,
not scared Paul really means to sell the place.
I see him through the kitchen window now,
sunk in thought, gazing at the frozen lake—
not eager for our company, I'm sure.
What answers will that cold, blue crystal give him?

I'm bracing for the worst, although his mind
and mood could change, like thunderclouds that threaten
but drop no more than shadows. I must wait.
Still—I'm tired, Alice, *not* up for a fight
both lose if just one wins. I keep on hoping.
But winter lasts a long, long time up here.

Not Forgotten
—in memory of G. L.—

Call him a distant neighbor, this rare gent.
Some thought him moody, or at least reserved,
for he said no more than he truly meant.
For years we'd waved or nodded till he swerved,
one cold March day that found me on my roof,
and climbed the ladder up to knee-deep snow
he helped me clear. Aloft yet not aloof,
we traded quips as white mounds grew below,
then ventured tips to gauge each other's skill
at what he dubbed "the tricks of gardening."
We soon agreed on what and how to till,
and when we touched on food for plants in spring,
he pointed with the stem of his full pipe
at woodstove ashes spread along my drive.
"Fruit trees love them," he drawled, "but any type
of plant that craves potash will likely thrive."
Next growing season—and those ever since—
proved his advice. And so I sought to grace
him with best fruits for this and other hints
he sometimes dropped while pausing by my place.
If he had been a frequent passerby
or I more watchful for his rolling gait,
my plan, I'm sure, would not have gone awry.
Yet sudden death was his untimely fate—
as he had known it might be, one supposes.
He left small sums, I heard, no miser's stashes,
but instructions to enrich a bed of roses
beside the kitchen garden with his ashes.

Outside the Box: a Lone Dissenter

At a friendly gathering last week
I saw a man I might have been.
Well-groomed and -tailored, rather blinded
by fashion, he seemed absent-minded
yet comfortable in his skin.
He'd reached some goals I once aspired to—
while I'd asked not to be rehired, true.
The other guests had come to speak
smooth words of praise, perhaps to quote
some timeworn passage or recall
a tame and flattering anecdote.
These earnest speakers, great and small,
had like the man they honored toiled
long years within a lecture hall,
mined books for undiscovered gold,
and authored lengthy tomes which coiled
snakelike around the ore they guarded.
So as I heard tributes unfold,
it seemed, like piles of wool uncarded,
I longed to find in this recital
some thought, original and witty,
that hadn't perished in committee
and might have shown a man more vital.
He, meanwhile, who I might have been
with perfect calm took it all in.

Yet as talk dragged, I felt more pity
for all concerned with their school's scheme—
this modern, treeless academe.
I'd trusted my own intuition,
making a wild and reckless choice
to live an older, earthbound mission
that let me keep and train my voice.
Deep resonance of mountain brooks

drowned out dry, tone-deaf notes in books.
I learned, and not through textbook theory,
ethereal music from a veery.
No ponderous speech matched golden tones
of tulip-trees' high, silent cones.
No leaves of print could make me sing
as maples' green glow does in spring,
or touch the chords of autumn's grief
more surely than each flaming leaf.
From higher learning's walls I broke
to probe wild orchids by an oak,
and kept faith with this outdoor school
deliberately to find a way
to know the world, and not to rule
more than my true sense night and day.

At last all talking ceased. Awhile
I lingered, thinking of the smile
back then on the man I might have been
before our contact had grown thin.
The speeches I had listened to
revealed a figure of some merit
whose work, if not profound or new,
might more than dust on shelves inherit—
yet needed books to rescue it,
and they were hardly Holy Writ.
So I little cared what once he meant,
what now still less; nor would repent
the path I'd traveled, all I did,
and could still do—as from the back
of the empty room two men in black
advanced and closed his coffin-lid.

Walking into History

A fair May day remains the best excuse
to set old lust to wander on the loose—
made keener by a tantalizing tip
a white-haired friend had recently let slip.
She guessed two foragers could not resist
one taste of spring most of the world has missed,
on a Catskill shelf she might not see again.
That steep trail—one foot higher for every ten
my love and I walked forward—brought us through
a forest floored in violets of each hue
we knew and more we didn't, or a raft
of trilliums strewn so widely that we laughed
with glee, or then the soundless bells wild oats
swung while we heard a hermit thrush's notes.
Still other blossoms shone to claim our eyes,
and for two winding miles we'd slowly rise
with squirrel corn and Dutchman's-breeches, blooms
of blue cohosh and still-green Solomon's-plumes.
Yet as we praised wildflowers we came upon,
at length we wondered if our prize was gone—
had vanished like the spots from last year's fawn.
"O ye of little faith," we later said
quite sheepishly, as one short climb ahead
we saw enough ramps for a proper feast
and paused for breath. But pulses had increased
and would not calm down till a large supply
of wild leek bulbs and leaves had been laid by.
We rested then and washed our digging tools
in cold spring water trickling into pools
too handy to be there by accident.
We'd made good use of some rude settlement

(it dawned on us) not yet entirely lost;
and as the pungent scent of fresh ramps crossed
with coffee saved from lunch, we felt at heart
the living past in which we played a part.
Our friend advised us better than she knew,
perhaps; although it might be just as true
that her sly hint had led us on to see
and recognize this human history.
Yes, it made sense, however slightly planned;
seasoned foot-travelers would understand:
discovering gifts left by new and old springs
to find how versed they are in country things.

The Brotherhood
—for Raymundo Rodriguez-Jackson—

Spiderlings fling silk threads
on taut clotheslines, loose fences,
doors of my barn and sheds
with no polite pretenses
about just who owns what:
they're caught up in their spinning.
I'll bring my human But
and aging underpinning
into their lives as soon
as dew begins to dry
and, whistling an old tune
while passing one strand by,
I stroll into another:
unmissable disaster
for one small Earthly brother
whose blundering web-master
I simply can't help being.
Our paths will always cross.
That's not to say I'm freeing
myself of gain from loss:
his fiber sticks to me,
I know, and all too plainly.
Could he and I agree,
once, how we're bound: not mainly
as friend or enemy,
light loser and dark winner,
wee saint against large sinner,
but each his own line-spinner.

The Human Element

I walked along a Great Lake's ancient cliffs,
dotted with harebells and scrub mountain ash
and lit by lichens' orange hieroglyphs.
Together we enjoyed the spume and crash
of cold blue waves damping September's sun,
sunk halfway to its winter home down south,
but with a sultry week or two to run
before rains came to break the grip of drouth.
Then at my feet a small and moister cranny
barely revealed a gentian in full bloom:
still, delicate, light-purple lobes—uncanny
amid a bed of rocks and breakers' boom.
I had no doubt the plant had chosen well
to spend its life adorning a wild shore,
and hoped its striking flowers might cast their spell
upon these cliffs and skies forevermore.
Yet two steps farther on I found each flower
plucked from a larger plant of this closed gentian.
Its power to charm is great, but greater power
to waste had paid its beauty cruel attention.

The Stairway to Heaven

"Look, Frank! the full moon's rising from the lake."

"I didn't know Superior gave birth
to moons as well as huge lake trout and walleyes."

"Come see the big pumpkin for yourself, silly.
It's over half-way up; you're missing it!"

"I'm almost done with this fern article.
A minute more…hey! don't turn off the lights.
Did you just flip the cabin's circuit breakers?
Oh, I give up. All right, I'm coming, Ruth—
if I don't stumble on the furniture."

"You won't. Moonlight's flooding the living room."

"My gosh, it *is* a pumpkin."

                        "Giant orange—
and well-kissed by the sun—seems more apt, though,
now that it's round and poised above the water.
And extra lighting spoils the whole effect."

"The great outdoors is pretty well lit, yes.
Moonbeams have made a trail right to our dock."

"Said like a true landlubber. My grandfather—"

"The brave Norwegian sailor—"

                        "You mean captain.
He always called it the stairway to heaven:
waves glisten and guide your eyes up to the moon.

I don't know where he got the notion from.
Maybe himself: the old salt was a poet.
But what you said intrigues me now, Frank: why
should those stairs be one-way?"

                    "And to a dead moon.
No bliss or joy except the frozen type,
like human figures on an antique vase."

"No feeling that a heaven's possible—
or knowable except by us on Earth."

"How rarely true that is in practice, though.
I'd say Earth's far more like old-fashioned hell,
for you especially: one great gift crushed
by some drunk driver, and your right hand's gone,
never again to dance through Chopin's waltzes
or brave Beethoven's finger-busters—"

                        "Stop!
This arm with no hand screams 'Where!?' every time
I flex. It's hard enough to bear. At least
I played for people ten years—and world-wide.
Let's leave it there."

                  Clouds plunged the scene in darkness.
But moonlight slipped through moments later, gleaming
on tear-lined cheeks. A silver-haired man, head
down, stood nearby.

            "Besides—need I remind you?—
one listener, a botany professor—"

"Just-tenured then, who'd taught himself to play
the violin—"

        "Convinced me in six weeks—"

"Bright student—"

                "Life with him was worth long months
apart we knew our jobs would ask of us.
And homecomings turned into honeymoons."

"Too short during school years. My students must
have guessed that some exams let me play hooky.
The sins of my wild youth!"

                "At forty-three?"

"Still, what surprised me most about those trysts
was how much time we *didn't* spend in bed.
I thought you had to be joking with me—
asking to see new test plots of wildflowers."

"I told you I grew up on a small farm."

"I found out what that meant: you knew the names—
a few in Latin—of nearly every plant,
including some outside the study's fences,
from spotted coral root to blue-eyed grass."

"My mother's gift to me—from all our walks
around the farm, starting when I was two.
You brought them back like bursts of second blooms.
One flower ramble in particular,
through grassy marshes—you remember?"

                "Yes…
that August afternoon—before we married—"

"I saw—or did you see it first?—"

                "Maybe…"

"*We* saw a purple-fringed orchid. And then,
as we knelt for a closer look, your eyes
showed me the prize I'd always hoped to find:
not just the flower's reflection, but down deep
the whole man blossoming. That made me yours.
I haven't whispered this secret till now,
twenty-two Augusts since the quiet fact.
Yet even if it's only moonlight's spell
freeing my tongue, the simple truth remains:
we *are* soul-mates—heaven enough for me."

Moonlight profiled weathered facial landscape
Frank averted slowly, eyes now darkened.

"Dear Ruth! you tell me more about myself
than this old freethinker would dare to wish for.
I wonder if I'm worthy of your vision.
The scientist in me scoffs at every leap
of faith past Mother Nature—anyone's.
But I'm a fiddle-player, too, a man
who loves and tries to make a music you
enchant me with, despite—no, no, because
of all you've suffered. Can you understand?
I'm not sure I do. First you dazzled me,
like some new keyboard at your fingertips—
even inspiring me to test my hands
and nameless fiddle with Bach's great Chaconne.
I gamely sawed away until it dawned
on me I had far more fun listening."

"Yes...wasn't it, oh, fifteen years ago?"

"Try twenty—*I'd* almost forgotten, too.

Your accident was years off. Then it came,
shattering the sound world we took for granted.
But music's in you, so you practice, struggle.
I don't know if it comforts you."

                      "Sometimes."

"And yet—to my ears—your touch keeps its gold.
One evening last month, though—at home before
we came up to the shore—I overheard
raw passion rouse the Bechstein's voice again,
with that Chaconne—the version for left hand
Brahms made, his tribute to the masterwork.
Gripping the back door I eavesdropped, transfixed:
caught by close harmonies of grief and joy.
You took me to a higher realm, in tears."

"Dear man! now I feel what you meant—and mean."

That feeling staggered them, the moon made clear.
Locking luminous eyes, they steadied themselves
and gently joined their forms for one long kiss.

"When the last chord faded, I couldn't bear
to talk or intrude, so I took a walk
and thanked my lucky stars for you in silence.
But moonlight's made me spill my secret, too.
I don't know where its stairway leads except
to lovers' eyes and hearts. It always has."

"Tonight it's there for ours. Let's celebrate
the rarest way, my love, and bathe in it."

"You don't mean—"

"Yes. 'Uncommon warmth this summer,'
the neighbors told me. So I checked. They're right:
a record temperature—and nearly calm.
We'll never have a better chance than this."

"Then by the light of the silvery moon,
come float with me up heaven's shining stairs."

October Daybreak

The way dawning light
gilds these maples, this birch
transfigures fall's might,
builds a steeple and church.

Autumn Farewell

That day fading rays
climb fall's treetops and skies
to ignite one last blaze
primes the dew in rapt eyes.

A Leaf for Hardwoods

Gone, all gone—the wild blaze that was October
has left a land in ashes, stone-cold sober.
It seems impossible that not one leaf
has dried and dropped to earth consumed by grief,
or that the loss felt keenly on my side
no hardwood skeletons have magnified.
For woods are open to a piercing view
denied in summer by the green work crew
which fed and clothed until it fell from, tattered,
the skyward-stretching bones that always mattered.
And how they stand does not make me downcast.
I think back to the pasture of years past
when skinny seedlings proved their pent-up vigor
as oaks and maples thinned grass and grew bigger;
then to March sap runs and footprinted miles
in snow to gather pails from dripping spiles;
or two-by-fours milled from a stand of ash
to build a shed, the perfect firewood cache.
Yet hardwoods mean more for their well-built selves,
as anyone who dwells with them and delves
into the record of their cores will learn.
For they possess the art of sure return
from winter graves which humankind, with vaster
control of earthly lives, has failed to master.
What rare souls might from afterlife expect
is no crown, trunk, and limbs to resurrect
but only well-made leaves, whose borrowed breath
recalls their maker's mind and heart from death.
True, nothing and no one escapes that night
at last; yet leaf trees make so much of light

that in bare, darker times they can play dead.
No idle boast, it's what they've done, not said,
which turned heads so imagination roves
through every season free in hardwood groves.

Clear and Cold

A certain winter light
enacts an ancient rite.
It makes no pretty speech
yet what it tells may teach
those now within its lines
of sight how it refines.
The natural child of frost,
it clarifies what's lost:
brief beauty's final cost.
It burns through haze and mist
silently to insist
on forms just as they are—
young and old, near and far.
Even clad in ice or snow
they're clearly lit to show
what's gone or going fast,
and what's been built to last.
This nearly second sight
makes cold truth art in spite
of longest, darkest night.

In a Black Birch Grove

Tall pillars growing old in talus,
your bark is cracked, but it won't fail us
who wander in this native church
you built for patient, inward search.
I haven't come to swing a tree
toward hidden heaven or lost youth,
or to penetrate your mystery
more deeply than the simple truth
of atmosphere you grace me with
in snapped twigs' sap and fragrant pith
made somehow from thin, acid soil.
I come to breathe sweet, unburned oil
on stony sanctuary ground:
cool wintergreen incense year round.

Going for Gaywings

At first brown leaves were all I saw
alongside Potterville's old road.
Well, early May'd been fairly raw,
and April twenty-fourth it snowed.
That white stuff didn't stick, of course,
but the timing made me wonder then
if summer'd take the land by force
and jump the calendar again.
Spring's often *sulky* hereabouts,
too, pouting in rainclouds and mist
till lazy sunshine dries downspouts
yet won't stop frost—you get the gist.
I sighed and started to walk on
while glancing at the brown roadside
where a dot the shade of rosy dawn
stopped me. Dead leaves had failed to hide
the flower bud that made me peer
for more, or flowers open wide.
Just buds I spied. But never fear,
I thought: these woods are well-supplied
with other treats. I'd have a look
at blooming shadbush, stroll a spell
in the company of this trout brook,
and maybe rose-pink dots would swell.

Now, for shad blossoms—and new bronze
of beech leaf-buds—I walked a mile
or so; and then I found coiled fronds
of fiddleheads for lunch. Meanwhile
the sun showed up for work near noon
and stayed till dusk, which meant my story
grew brighter too; for pretty soon,
towards three o'clock, I got my quarry.

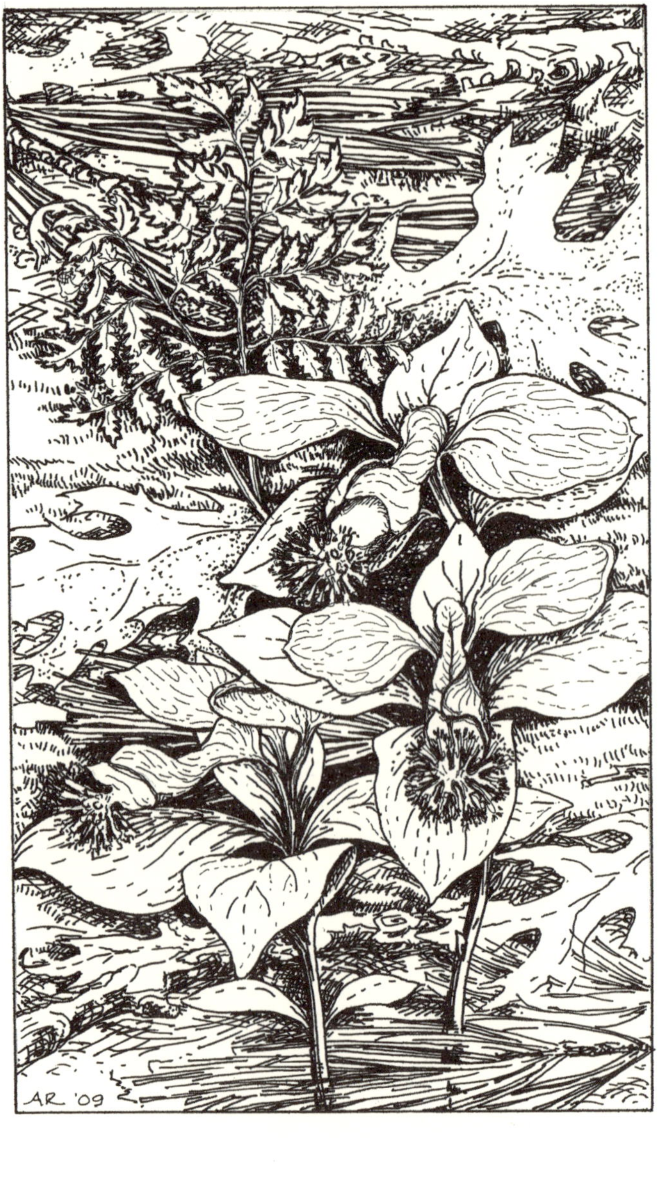
AR '09

Those dots of pink I'd seen before
had blossomed, basking in full sun;
old-timers seeing May's woodlot floor
named them gaywings in harmless fun.
I'd come to spot their latest landing,
though missing how these forest-dwellers
first flew in—past my understanding.
Still, inch-long wings joined to propellers
do make a most unusual sight
that's brought me back for umpteen springs.
I can't pass up this cherished rite
of May, or of slow wanderings
away from a world now so far gone
with being new at any cost
and headlong speed. I'm sooner drawn
to simpler pleasures getting lost.

I see your smile. But if you think
I'm just a sentimental fool
chasing wildflowers dressed in hot pink,
go see if you don't lose your cool.
Their charms are older than our race
and were so memorably designed
as to wipe that smile right off your face.
I dare you: they'll stick in your mind.

Summoning Eliza

I am the quiet one—so my friends say—
as if you, my Cherokee grandma, told them.
You knew me better, though. With you I didn't
always hold my tongue, and then your eyes,
big and dark brown, stared hard at me, unblinking.
Sometimes they filled with tears of grief or joy,
because you got the truth I spared all others.
Remember us, there on your big front porch
in summer, snapping beans while trading secrets,
or singing tribal tunes by heart at dusk?
I think back even more to those old tales
you spun and wove—well laced into my mind:
some sad ones suffered on the Trail of Tears;
some celebrating great Sequoyah's script,
whose characters keep voices singing strong.
How many times I've thought of you, Eliza,
while soaking in this brook and washing up
below its waterfall in my back yard!
You never saw it, but your spirit's here,
I know, in mountain water's endless song.
I'm glad your rare, old-fashioned name's mine, too,
surviving like a throwback to lost virtues;
my folks knew somehow that their baby birl
whose skin mixed cream and coffee might just be
a gardener and forager like Grandma
and live as far from pavement as she did.
How right they were! I bloomed into your ways.
My husband Ben's like-minded, always was;
he grew up camping, as he likes to say,
and learned to read wilderness like a poem.
He guides less privileged people—caged in cities
except two short weeks each year—back to where
they find a world they can't quite do without.

We weren't tempted by their god of Progress:
improving Nature by strip-mining it
and strewing tailings that make it worse still.
We stayed where food is what we grow ourselves
or take from woods and fields; sun, wind, and water
power us and won't stop soon or cost a cent;
and fun is what we dream up living here.
I don't dream much in stone-chilled water, though;
it keeps me focused on things as they are:
my bulging belly floating high, for instance.
In one month, maybe less, my man and I
will have another wanderer to feed
and guide through those green years we've left behind.
Too far behind? our gray hair made us ask,
and doubt shot arrows deep into our minds.
We fought with words as strong as heavy blows,
but in the end our souls obeyed one passion,
thrilled and stilled alone by putting in seed.
The little sprout has grown well in my soil
and kicks hard like the boy we know he is;
the rest's a mystery only time will solve.
We hope this corner of real Earth we love
will capture his heart, too: sign-language shown
by turkey prints in snow, new trillium leaves
unfurling in April sunshine, sweet scent
that pinkster sends while hiding in the woods.
And if the music of this unspoiled land—
from our own brook and waterfall and songs
of hylas, hermit thrushes, and horned owls
to winter's moans and long, deep silences—
if these wild wonders stir his lasting wonder,
he can't and won't be satisfied with less.
From where I float in water as cold as truth,
I don't see why he'd choose another way;
but trying to sidestep old Mother Nature

has been man's game too long for me to doubt
our race will ever give up hope of winning.
Do people really win by cheating Nature?
Their lives are journeys their souls fear to take,
it seems to me—except on safe, rigged terms.
What folly! Life's the trip they can't help taking,
whether they stay at home or try globe-trotting.
And your imagined voyages, Eliza—
all questing minds'—have leapt past time and space,
creating afterlives in memory.
My son, I trust, won't lose *his* mind group-thinking,
but use grandmother wit that's in his genes.
Yet it is fitting that the love and wisdom
you made your own took second place to guts,
the one way our old planet hasn't changed:
raw courage is the virtue which counts most.
You knew and lived this well, Eliza, dear;
so that's my deepest wish for him: to know
in his own bones, wherever he may wander—
on paths he wants to walk or dares to build—
foot-worthy trails are made by thought and grit.

Mother of All Change

We're right to call the Earth our mother—
though sometimes wishing for another,
whose will and moods we might foretell
or even steer toward heaven, not hell.
Has she longed for the same, I wonder,
and ranked us as a growing blunder—
too willful, moody, with raw talents
for power enslaving reason, balance?
It's clear who'll win this tug-of-war,
but cooler heads should mind the score.
For mankind's masses churn out heat
that's melting many a vast ice sheet:
a home truth Mother Earth has spoken—
the louder as more ice is broken.
Her meaning? Leaders disagree,
and force us all to wait and see.
Yet as she speaks at length world-wide
about this human aftermath,
her tone is not in doubt—and I'd
be ready for revolt and wrath.

The New Age of Dinosaurs

I haven't yet laid eyes upon the beasts,
but signs of them are strewn across the planet:
land gouged and eaten in huge, endless feasts;
tall temples built of steel, concrete, and granite.
Their human slaves, in lifelong sacrifice,
toil on to please the soulless omnivores,
consuming at an ever-rising price
all that the wide world grows or makes or stores.

"Earth's our commodity!"—their constant hymn—
controls the great globe's spin, it seems, for now.
The code-named monsters, some by acronym,
pray on with prophets sacred to their Dao.
And when they waste their habitat at last,
they'll make a meal of money. Then they'll fast.

Survivors

Our battered plum tree's coming into bloom.
Two branches got emergency rough-pruning
March forced on us in its wild, icy gloom.
House finches, wrens, and robins won't be tuning
up there again. And who knows when or if
those shortened arms might beckon with sound growth
to thirsty mason bees, but just stay stiff,
stump-like? We still hope, yet we'd take no oath
that shoots now sprouting from cracked, scaly bark
will ever blossom much or hold thrush singers.
At least my love and I were here to aid
the tree when ice shined, though its power was dark.
A larger death we've stayed, perhaps. What lingers
in fragrant flowers signs life's vow we three made.

A Tough Old Native
—*for Ann and Dan Guenther—*

Three leaflets caution, "Touch me not!" and mean it—
though this whole thing from flowers to hairy roots
plagues careless wanderers who wish they'd seen it.
But all the hungry birds that eat its fruits
and spread seeds may give those same people pause
to wonder how a brainless plant's so clever:
for them enacting one of Nature's flaws
while doubling to help birds survive—however.

The plain truth is mankind was not the point,
for this old vine grew long before its hour.
Nor has our young, proud race with all its tools
yet made, lifewise, the *necessary* joint
with Nature, bending or fulfilling rules
to equal poison ivy's staying power.

The Herb Witch

Is that you, Henry? Ah, I hear you now,
tapping H-E-N-R-Y in Morse Code.
Come in and have a cup of nettle tea,
you clever devil: good for your hay-fever.
And how's your mother? Not so well, you think?
What's wrong? Slow down there, young man. These old eyes
can't follow sign-language when you're excited.
Oh, my. She fell and twisted her bad ankle.
I'm sorry. Poor Martha! But otherwise
she's all right? Good. Now, where'd I put the comfrey?
Here, Henry. See this gauze bag of dried leaves?
Tell your mother to boil it for five minutes,
lift the bag out with tongs and let it cool
a bit, then wrap it warm onto the swelling.
Should last twelve hours and could be re-boiled once.
But use a new bag each day; there, take two more.
They ought to help. Your mother's fresh tomatoes
will be payment enough—if she can spare them.
My goodness, now that you're closer I see
you'll need a comfrey compress for that shiner!
How did the bruise below your eye get there?
Some bigger, older lads yelled "Mother's boy,"
I see, pushed you, forced you to fight, and boom!
knocked you down. Ah, this note's for me to read:
"I had a scrap with my contemporaries
because they called my mom a name that rhymes
with what I've always heard them call you—witch.
Neither is true, I know, and so I fought."
Bless you, young man; I see it all too clearly.
Let's take care of that nasty black-and-blue.
You know, home-schooling hasn't hurt your English;
your cruel contemporaries' isn't half

as good—and you are only ten years old.
Not till next month, is it? Remarkable!
As for my nickname—yes, even before
dear Mr. Gardner passed on I was known,
and with affection, as the old herb witch.
Now here I am, twenty-three years a widow,
my good trade name darkened by age alone.
People have buried me before I'm dead!
A healthy ninety-one-year-old's beyond
their small imaginations—airtight boxes.
Just hold still while I put the compress on.
Not too warm, Henry? Fine. Well, you must know
I've struggled with contemporaries, too.
They wish I wouldn't think or speak so freely.
The First Church of Cranberry, Scientist,
I used to say, half-joking, for a rise.
You're smiling, Henry. Sometimes they would chuckle,
so I'd push harder, saying I preferred
to know the god I kneeled to touch and taste
was real and not some otherworldly ghost.
Besides (I'd add if they still played along)
those worlds in outer space don't have our life—
and mighty cold the gaps between them, filled
with deadly rays no human could survive.
Loud laughs or forced smiles told me where I stood;
today I daren't tweak the tender souls.
What's that, Henry? Yes, people disagreed.
I heard them out, and kept an open mind.
The ones who really irked me were so cocksure—
like smug high priests of modern medicine.
To me *their* science is "alternative."
Believing it's our cure-all is pure hubris.
You understand that antique Greek word, Henry?

I see you do: "Pride makes them learned fools."
Bravo, you witty young philosopher!
I don't copy their silly claims, but give
my old way credit when it helps a person.
Life is more art than science, anyway;
the young M.D. I sometimes see admits it.
At least he's willing to think past pill bottles.
Done with your tea, Henry? Let's check that bruise.
Those ruffians should be ashamed: attacking
a nine-year-old who can't call out for help!
You'd better keep the bandage on, my friend.
It's not pretty, but neither is this swelling;
and both are trifling to the ugly habit
of picking on people who are different:
that all-too-human, inbred cruelty
of normal folks. Be glad you're not called witch.
Don't be afraid to be yourself, though, Henry.
Your mind's a match for any boy's brainpower,
take it from me: I've seen a long life's-worth.
Your mother must be proud—speaking of whom,
I've got the bulk of what she ordered here:
dried pennyroyal, slippery elm bark,
and recipes for early nettle greens.
The rest I'll have next week, if that's all right.
Be careful now, dear boy, on your way home—
two miles, I'd guess, by bike from my outskirts
to your place near the village's inskirts.
Two-and-a-half, is it? You make a detour
to use the library, either for study
or refuge, sometimes both. I get the point.
You know what it means to live by your wits,
don't you? Be sure to give your mom a hug
along with home-grown herbs from Great-Aunt Rachel.

Looking after Wild Wallflowers

Ah, why'd I ever dream I'd weed this wall?
Just look! the very stones are bound in thrall
to root claws clasping every crack and cranny.
No one can weed and let the wall stand, can he?
I'll set a limit on what must come out
and what stays put (and will) through floods and drought.

I can't cut milkweed: it's for butterflies,
or bees to raid and leave with bulging thighs.
And it's no weed like multiflora rose
that spreads too well and starts a runny nose.
No critter but a finch would miss these thistles,
yet then I'd get no golden guided missiles
come late fall when most color's moldy ground
with little save witch hazel blooms around.
There's poison ivy I won't dare to touch;
still, chipping sparrows might—to feed a clutch
of hatchlings—airlift berries left behind
in raw spring—winter's way of being kind.
(But not to me or earth beneath a nest
where birds plant seeds they never quite digest.)
And here's a patch of thickly growing myrtle,
so rampant that you'd swear the wall's as fertile
as compost piles. Where should I start to trim
what blooms in spring on nothing but a whim
and, glistening in bursts of sun through sprinkles,
turns ravishing, a blaze of periwinkles?
These trumpet-flowers of blue and blushing pink—
too pretty to be called bindweed, I think—
I will disturb, but just to contemplate
tomorrow when light warms the wall at eight,

and sunbeams name each flower a morning-glory.
One day soon frost will make them all quite hoary,
weeding in one fell swoop. Many an aster
and myrtle leaf, I know, survive this plaster,
perhaps the next; yet flowers at last do go,
and leaves, though green, must wear thick coats of snow.

Meanwhile I'll pull enough encroaching vetch
to sit a spell here on the wall's home stretch,
considering the work I've left undone.
Most of these plants aren't hurting anyone,
in truth, and those unfit for human use
will always hide seeds somewhere on the loose.
Besides, their hold on this old land's as strong
as mine—much stronger when I think how long
they bloomed before the first plow turned its soil.
Instead of dwelling on the fruitless toil
of weeding out what dearly loves this wall,
I'll pick *flowers* with my eyes from spring through fall
and make the job joy's labor after all.

The Silver Squeak

A bird known for its needle bill
patrols my gardens with a will
before the August sun or I
have looked long at the morning sky.
No patient stalker like a heron,
it darts to sip each opening bloom,
madly circling a rose of Sharon.
Sober or not, it may soon zoom
to take deep draughts of new-made wines
from orange spouts on trumpet vines.
And then the sprite, quite drunk on summer,
zips off to blossoms of bee balm,
becoming their most thorough plumber.
Not tame or shy, without a qualm
the tiny tippler threatens me
if I disturb its drinking spree.
Its wings hummed nearer than four feet
once, as to say, "Just who in hell's
the owner of these coral bells?"
I heard the curse, and in retreat
marked well *his* gleaming ruby throat—
lost farther off as a bright dust mote.
I hope it won't seem odd or strange
that only at this point-blank range
could I be sure I'd roused male rage.
With such birds of uncertain age
it's hard to tell their men from women—
like spotting fast a ripe persimmon.
Whichever sex, they're on a binge
all day: it's what they're living for.
But as they drink on with no twinge
of guilt, one fact they can't ignore:

some flower-bars' early closing times
will send the feisty creatures roaming
for late drinks past my dinner chimes
but not (so far) beyond the gloaming.
Next morning I won't need to look
(and can't yet) through dawn's merest crack
to know that in a flowery nook
at least one thirsty drinker's back,
impatient with night's long intrusion
on a necessary blood transfusion.
I'll hear high-pitched notes, rather weak
though not because the singer's meek
but small, and chatters out of pique.
Sighing, I'll smile at the silver squeak.

Leaf Dancer

The gully-washer broke the drought too late
to save more than changed shades of autumn leaves,
whose brittle rustling sang the bitter fate
of stunted cornstalks no hands bound in sheaves.

One parched red maple leaf fell from a tree
swaying hard by a plunging brook's sheer height,
then flew upstream—as though by trickery
defying for a while that muddy white.

Twice more it took the stage to dance and float
above leaping water roaring in wrath
that filled a kettle-hole's deep, churning throat.
The paper dancer found this final bath,
I guessed, yet never saw that cavity
engulf what came to play with gravity.

By a Frozen Pond

The fox's snow-prints sharply turned to pass
stiff cattails mirrored by the foot-thick glass.

We paused from following the fresh fox-trot
to scan the silent pond and nearby swamp
and thought of last June's promise, autumn's pomp—
all crushed by ice upon this very spot.

We little hoped to flee the cold, vague beauty
which white-draped sculptures showed us everywhere,
and which had only done its yearly duty
to hide or camouflage each lodge and lair.

Nor did we yearn for summer's frenzied race
through its inheritance of green and gold—
too fast for most wild spendthrifts to grow old
before they join gray shades so commonplace.

We rather took in stride the snow-world's speed
that mastered ours and gave a greater worth
to silence. Yet, as people will when freed
by calm, we daydreamed, gazing at still earth,

of song that waits close by the frozen mirror
long muffling earth-tones till spring's lucky crack.
For while the shattered shine melts back to black
that pent-up music will resound the clearer

as out of slowly thawing muck and mire
rise silver voices of spring peepers' choir.

A Small White Hope
—*for Mary Catherine Fletcher, née White*—

I've seen it, so I know it's true—
though after drifts of white we've had
it's winter's joke more than spring's clue,
this blooming snow that makes me glad.

It can't stop frost, bone-chilling rain,
or April storms with real, wet snow;
and yet I know deep in the grain
what stirred from sleep has lit shadblow.

The small tree seems a humble token,
but signals far with each new blossom
that winter's grip is nearly broken
and spring no longer can play possum.

Earth-Centered

The universe was born in violence,
they say, and will in darkest rage go hence.
Yet out of all that lifeless, starry rubble
arose by slimmest chance a living bubble
which owned its share of old celestial war
but also reason's lights, hard to ignore:
the beam of science smiting superstition,
the poet's gleam inviting intuition—
mankind's gifts in the bubble's lasting fight
against primeval forces of the night.
As human seed who likewise beat long odds
to live, then witness ever more that prods
this sensitive sphere, I'm moved to use the wit
and time Earth granted me to sing for it.

Stayed by Stars

Something we shared, love, early this July
has stayed with me, and may have caught the eye
of heaven, blue and deep and radiant.
It wasn't just quick fingers in the hunt
for huckleberries, pursed lips for half-croons
whistling back yellowthroat and towhee tunes,
or careful footwork, oftener concealed
by bushes and tall grass in that old field,
lush from long ages of a mountain's breeding.
It was, set free, two pairs of eyes *joined*, reading
wild-blooming mysteries of whorled loosestrife,
that told a world about one man and wife
who kneeled by many a tiny Earth-made star
shining on them, showing how lucky they are.

A Flower for All Gardens
—*for Sadeth Everson Schley*—

You'd never doubt that one wildflower of all
that find their ways inside a garden wall
did not drop in or fly or creep or crawl

but came to be there by a human hand
perhaps in answer to that soul's demand
for beauty, use, or both upon his land.

This might spring from wake-robin's woodland show,
arbutus scent which rises as old snow
is melting, or wind playing with shadblow.

I've seen it happen when a columbine
once caught the climbing sun at half-past nine
and eyes that glowed and said, "This must be mine."

Or it may come about when a great drift
of Dutchman's-breeches tempts someone to lift
a few and carry off a well-clad gift.

And it may be, contrariwise, a leaf
shaped like a heart which is the lure, in brief,
of violets to make a flower-thief.

Yet I'm most fond of flowers wild places lent
not when they were the reason that I went
but left to live with me by accident—

as when a narrow path had forced my boots
to crush a long herb carpet to the roots
and made small, aromatic blooms and shoots

release perennial perfume I knew
from liberally seasoned beef ragout
or, even better, savory lamb stew.

And so those flowers that suffered my footfall
yet rose to tell their potent truth now call
a patch of ground I gave them home and sprawl

at leisure, as a lifelong paying guest
who knows his worth and will stay on with zest
well after I lie down for one last rest.

A gardener in that distant world may quarrel
with roses I loved, cut back mountain laurel,
move raised beds, thin asparagus or sorrel;

may spurn, in fact, my old-style paradigm
and curse the hard work I've bequeathed; but I'm
sure he'll wish I had left him still more thyme.

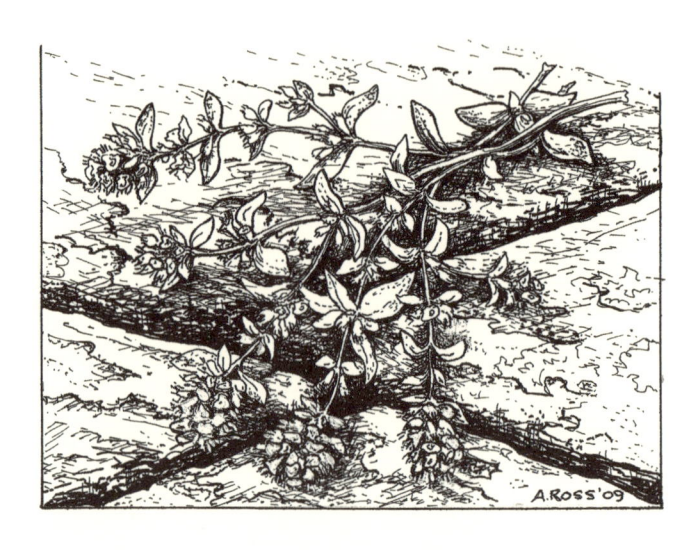

About the Author and the Illustrator

The singing line has long been and remains a way of life for New Paltz poet Roger Roloff, whether on the world's opera and concert stages during the nineteen-eighties and -nineties as Wagner's shoemaker-poet Hans Sachs and as baritone soloist in Vaughan Williams's *Dona Nobis Pacem*, or in his own previous poetry collections and the compact disc of new and selected works, *Natural Voice*. Offstage and -page he and his wife, musicologist Barbara Petersen, practice home-grown organic thrift: they tend wild and cultivated land which sustains them in tonic and dominant ways. It is only natural that this deep bond should find musical expression in *Illuminations*.

Anne S. Ross lives and works on her family's horse farm in Center Cambridge, New York. This beautiful agricultural region near the Vermont border is a constant inspiration for her artistry. Her days are filled with farm chores and pleasures, studio time, home-schooling, and the many joys of family. Anne works in pen and ink, watercolor, acrylic and pastel. She exhibits her artwork locally and from her studio.